Autumn Epiphany

GARETH PRICE

This book is dedicated to

Jill Mary Price (1940 – 2002)
Alan John Price (1935 – 2018)

their faith was evident all along

CONTENTS

"…but those who hope in the LORD will renew their strength.
They will soar on wings like eagles;
they will run and not grow weary,
they will walk and not be faint."

Isaiah 40.31

1 ST. MARY'S CHURCH

Between Goring and Streatley, the path north along the Thames switches from the east to the west bank, from Oxfordshire to Berkshire.

Once you've crossed over the bridge, admired the braided river making its way sedately south, the next fingerpost is a bit further along than expected, up Streatley High Street on the corner of Church Lane. The racing-green sign has an old-fashioned feel in keeping with this part of the Home Counties - an acorn, an arrow, and 'Thames Path – National Trail' painted on in a simple, fifties-style font.

And here, beneath seemingly cloudless skies on a Saturday morning in the middle of October, a group of runners and supporters are quietly, unhurriedly assembling; following their instructions to gather outside the Morrell Room (1), Streatley's brick and flint 19th century village hall.

There's an air of excitement and optimism, those taking part in the race immediately obvious, set apart by their apparel – running shoes, figure-hugging backpacks and small, squarish numbers pinned to their shorts.

At the end of the lane, a man in a red hoodie is

positioning a couple of portable Centurion banners to create a makeshift start line.

As the minutes tick by towards nine o'clock, more and more runners are arriving, and the congregation swells to a couple of hundred people. I distract myself by making conversation with those nearby.

There's a Scottish lady and her partner, excited about the fact she's starting her first ever hundred mile race.

I spy Ken Fancett, a slight, unassuming man in his seventies, much revered in these circles for completing more events with Centurion than anyone else (2), carrying the inquisitive, educated air of a Cambridge don. We get talking about Hilaire Belloc and 'The Old Way' along the North Downs; how those following the line of hills found their way across the Medway Gap in prehistoric times (3).

Over by the door to the hall, Gary Tuttle is stood with his wife. He's taking part in all eight races in 2022, the double 'Grand Slam', to raise money for the charity Tommy's after his "baby boy Orion was born sleeping at 40 weeks" (4). Despite entering four 50 milers, and four 100 milers in the space of seven months, he's somehow near the front of the field every time. And he's thrown in the London Marathon for good measure. Perhaps running is an outlet for his grief. Groupie-like, I shake his hand and tell him he's inspirational.

And finally here's Brian Drought, friendly and self-effacing as ever. He's open about the fact he hasn't done any training, and is happy just to be part of things, planning to call it a day after the first 25 miles. Probably.

Wiry and compact, James Elson, Race Director and founder of Centurion Running, arrives to conduct the race briefing. He's done this before, and is in obvious good humour, explaining his soft spot for the Autumn 100, "the last 100 miler of the season, a lovely little race". And having recently returned from completing the 220 mile Tor Des Géants ultra in the Italian Alps, with just the 86,000 feet of ascent, and a race time of 104 hours (5), I can see how he's landed on 'little'.

This also happens to be the only Centurion race James has taken part in rather than directed. Check the results for 2015 and you can see his name alone at the top of the leader board (6). First place in 14 hours, 35 minutes. Touché!

He encourages all those taking part in their first 100 miler to raise their hands, so we can give them an encouraging round of applause. Then all those aiming to complete the four race, 400 mile 'Grand Slam' get to raise their hands too. They receive a deferential round of applause.

The race is shaped like a cross. Four out-and-back legs, each approximately 25 miles in length, each ending at the village hall in Goring.

First up we'll head north along the Thames to Little Wittenham, then east along the Ridgeway to Swyncombe, west up the Ridgeway to Chain Hill, and finally, south-facing leg four follows the Thames Path down to Reading and back.

The weather forecast is good, and conditions are dry underfoot, perfect for trail running, and not surprising given the unusually dry start to the autumn. But, and it's a big but, we should be careful not to underestimate leg three. It's going to be blustery up there. For those slowing up, making their way onto the Ridgeway after dark, the windchill is going to make it feel very cold - so layer up.

We should watch out too when we cross the major roads, exercise due care and attention. There are a number of these hazards on the course and they won't be marshalled.

All too soon, a couple of in-jokes later, James has finished talking and it's nearly nine o'clock. Squeezed between the Morrell Room and a high wall a few feet away, the 234 race starters are compressed into a pre-Covid style pack. As everyone else edges forwards expectantly, I go against the grain, politely picking my way through to the back. There's no point in being anywhere else.

After not taking part in a race for over two years, I've kept faith in the idea of toeing the line in a hundred mile race for a third time. And as I strived for, and achieved my goal of running 1,000 miles in training in the six month build-up, visualising the pent up emotion of this pre-start experience has kept me going.

But now that I'm actually here, stood with my peers in these last moments before we head out, there's an empty feeling in the pit of my stomach, an unshakeable belief that I'll have to drop out at the first checkpoint at six miles, that my race is likely to be over virtually as soon as I start.

Up until three weeks before, all had gone reasonably accordingly to plan. I'd recovered from a slipped disc earlier in the summer and managed eight weeks of high volume running. This culminated in a seemingly successful recce weekend. Emily and I hung out in Streatley and Goring, and while she explored the shops in Wallingford, I checked out leg two on the Saturday, and leg three on the Sunday. I'd slowly covered 26.2 miles both days, and felt ready for the race (7).

But early on Sunday's effort I'd felt new pain in my right knee, and this worsened during the following week. On a routine visit to the chiropractor for more injections into the slipped disc, she diagnosed runner's knee, inflammation of the patella, normally healed through four to six weeks of complete rest. This was almost certainly caused by me changing to brand new shoes for the back-to-back marathon effort. Despite repeated and obsessive application of ice, in the last two and a half weeks before the race, any walking at all has felt painful. I called time on one foolhardy run after only five miles.

Three days out from the race I catch up with my sister Louise on Zoom. She spots the icepack on my knee, and once she's heard what has happened, questions whether it might be better not to start, to give it a chance to get better? 'There will be other races…'

I explain I'm signed up, we have the accommodation booked and I want to at least give it a go. I can drop out at the first checkpoint at Wallingford if needed, Emily will ensure I'm sensible. If by some miracle I do manage to keep going, any time inside 28 hours will do just fine, even if it means last place.

As the start hooter sounds and we begin to shuffle forwards together, there is a small but significant glimmer of hope - my newly rediscovered Christian faith; and, a conviction I've held since our Crowhurst weekend at the end of August, that I can honour God through my running. Despite almost overwhelming doubt about the state of my knee, when I'd got here about half past eight, I'd found some respite in a moment of silence at the end of the lane. Written across a wooden archway above the gate to St Mary's Church, were the words

'MY . PEACE . I . GIVE . UNTO . YOU'

Something I'd come to believe recently, was that in those moments of my life when I'd felt most lost or most in peril, despite my lack of faith, God had never abandoned me, he had been alongside me all along. Maybe this would be the same.

2 THE RIVER FINDHORN

I get a sense of foreboding as soon as I take my first few strokes. Something doesn't feel right.

I tell myself to dismiss it, that I've paddled the Findhorn seven or eight times before, that up until now, this morning has had a similar pattern to it to all the other kayaking trips.

We drove away from the bunkhouse, out through Strathspey into the middle of a sparsely populated part of the Highlands, windscreen wipers on full.

There was our first sighting of the Findhorn at Dulsie - adversarial, dark brown from the peat, running at a very high level. The others were excited, spurred on by the guidebook's description for the top section (8) – 'Good spate boating at Grade 3'. But to me at least, the old timer in the group, this was a classic 'grade three from the bridge' moment: when the rapid looks innocuous from a hundred feet or so above, but down in the middle of it, navigating from the cockpit of a small boat with just a paddle for protection, you can be sure it will be a lot more serious.

Back in the minibus we're soon making a left onto the final road to the get in, carefully negotiating a single track lane with grass in the middle.

Safely parked up in the layby, I stick my nose out of the van. There's more rain in the air, the smell of damp winter bracken, low cloud scuttling across the surrounding hills. I look around for a glimpse of lungwort, the lichen which grows on the trees up here, an indicator of clean air. But the others are keen to get going and I'm interrupted, called over to help untie the boats from the trailer. It's time to settle into preparing for the trip, following the series of rituals that have held me in good stead for the last 15 years or so...

Stow your throwline and dry bag, your food and warm clothes in alongside the buoyancy foam in the stern of the boat, clipping them securely to the back of the seat.

Fiddle with the footrest bolts so you can get it set at exactly the right place, six or seven holes from the end, then when you're snuggly wedged in, you'll be able to edge the boat with your knees. Dismiss the fact that inside the cockpit, it seems more cramped than it should be.

Change into your wetsuit, reaching round to zip up the back. Try to stay calm during that familiar moment of claustrophobia as you pull on your dry cag and the protective rubber seal snags on the top of your head making you feel trapped inside.

Apply wax to your Werner paddles so you can still grip the shaft in the bigger water, those moments when the river throws buckets of icy H2O in your face and chest.

Stuff the group's waterproof map securely inside your buoyancy aid...

And now I'm sat in the boat, attaching my neoprene deck at the back, reaching round behind me to make sure it's tucked beneath the rim all the way round, so I don't commit the schoolboy error of the whole thing pinging off as soon as I try and attach it at the front; making sure the grab loop, the mechanism for releasing the deck if I need to exit the boat in a hurry, is easily to hand.

Then I seal launch down the grassy bank and skid out onto the river, instinctively leaning into a low brace, resting my paddle on the surface of the water to prevent a capsize.

It's December 2008 and I'm nearing the end of my thirties. After 15 years of being an outdoor instructor, I've moved into a busy fundraising job, and this is my first outing for 12 months. I'm a stone heavier than last year and feel unease at the position of the boat, worryingly low in the water, not dissimilar to when it's swamped.

Soon everyone else has joined me, we're on our way, and already, there are butterflies in my stomach, a sense the river's moving too fast for me, that although we're not yet into the more technical section, the bank is speeding by and I feel disconcerted by my lack of control.

I decide to roll to sharpen things up, and splash water on the back of my neck, readying myself for the freezing December immersion. Upside down, I'm initially disorientated, waiting for the muscle memory to kick in. I tuck forwards, reaching for the surface above me, and sweeping round with the paddle and swinging my hips, I flip myself back up. There's the familiar 'ice cream head' in the aftermath, hilarity at my startled expression.

When I lost my Christian faith at the end of my teens, I still craved spiritual nourishment, a way of making sense of the world and my place in it. To a certain extent, I found it in the outdoors. Especially when, on my days off, I pushed myself to the edge of my ability in the mountains, climbing and canoeing, seeking the right companions, that sweet spot where I was at the outer limit of control, those moments where there was a sense of oneness with the river or the rock, the natural world.

This striving frequently took me up into Snowdonia. I remember the River Ogwen in particular, paddling with Keith in 1994 - early on, accelerating along the Gun Barrel, the fast moving channel above the double-step falls, being spun around on the first drop, and negotiating the second one backwards. In big water through Bethesda Gorge, I was buffeted towards the rock wall on the left, and instinctively leaned in, bracing off it with my paddle. Pumped with adrenaline, we paddled down the Grade Four Fisherman's Gorge in almost perfect sync with each other and the river, attacking rapid after rapid, feeling like we could tackle anything (9).

I graduated to the French Alps in 1997 and 2004, Guillestre the base, collecting intense memories of clear blue skies, the air temperature in the thirties, wild strawberries along the banks and powerful life affirming moments paddling glacial meltwater - Grade Three and Four rivers like the Clarée, Onde, and Ubaye.

The thing I loved about white water kayaking was that once you accelerate out of the eddy and break into the current, twisting into your bow rudder to spin downstream, there's very little time for fear or self-doubt. And when you react appropriately to the currents around you, you're in tune with the river, aligned with its force.

After portaging a Grade Six rapid on the Guisane in 1997, Keith and I paddled down an unexpectedly serious section of Grade Four river. We had no time to think, no chance to break out, there was only pure flow, a series of strokes and reactions as we paddled over drop after drop. When we finally found an eddy and came together again, we were whooping with joy from the exhilaration of it all.

Back on the Findhorn, I've come to a decision - discretion is the better part of valour - paddle over to the side and get out. Let the younger guys have their fun. Your heart's not in it any more. Walk your boat back to the minibus, and meet them at the bottom.

I spot an obvious eddy just downstream of a little drop and decide that's where I'll leave the group. I let the others know. But the river is still moving too fast for me. I've switched off too soon, and I'm on top of the drop before

I'm ready. Much too late, I realise it's an almost river-wide ledge, a not-in-the-guidebook natural weir. The pronounced horizon line offers a tell-tale sign there'll be a recirculating stopper, that all of the action, all the energy of the bankful river will be swirling around beneath the surface. Backpaddling frantically in vain, I drop into the slot at the base of the weir, the spot where two competing channels of water are dragging everything downwards with a great deal of force. I'm almost immediately flipped upside down.

I don't have my paddles any more. Disorientated and knowing I'm in big trouble I fumble around trying to pull my deck. Out of the boat I'm sucked down deep under the surface, wrenched this way and that like a ragdoll. There are churning bubbles everywhere and an eerie olive green translucence, almost all of the available daylight penetrating the surface.

There has always been paddlers' pub talk, stories of the friend of a friend, who when trapped in a recirculating stopper under a weir, counter-intuitively took off their buoyancy aid, so they could sink beneath the stopper and into the downstream flow of the river, which took them back to the surface, away from the danger. Now, when it comes to it, inside this washing machine, I don't have any time to think, I'm a long way short of this sort of affirmative action.

Eventually I do surface again. It's been 90 seconds or so and I'm gasping for air, facing upstream and being tugged inexorably back towards the slot. The river water is falling vertically over the weir, normally a sign that the recirculating stopper will be more powerful. Over to the right, I can see Steve, the Level Five Coach and most qualified member of our group. He's had the presence of mind to try and make it round the weir on the left hand side but he's still having to throw in a series of vigorous support strokes to stay upright.

In the last few moments before being pulled back into

the slot, I do have the chance to take a breath. I'm then sucked beneath the surface again. And this time, with my energy draining away, I feel even more helpless, thrown around by forces much greater than me. Maybe this is what it feels like to be mauled by a wild animal. At the mercy of the turbulence, the thought comes into my head that I'm not able to breathe down here, I haven't taken in any oxygen for a long time, and I may not come up again.

Sometime later I do break the surface. Further downstream this time and free from the grip of the stopper. My boat and paddles are nowhere to be seen. The current is carrying me rapidly down river, waves breaking over my head.

I become aware of an urgent, purposeful figure in my peripheral vision. It's Ben, leaning into the situation, paddling frantically to come and help me.

I reach for the grab handle on the end of his little boat as he shouts at me to swim for the side. Drained of energy from my time in the stopper, and aware for the first time of how very cold I feel, my tired half-hearted attempts at front crawl seem to be having no effect at all.

Ben is trying to nudge me with his boat, trying to push me in the direction of the bank, but the current is carrying us both downstream at a significant rate of knots. The river is winning the battle. I can't help remembering that somewhere ahead of us and approaching fast must be the bigger rapids we'd seen from Dulsie Bridge. He'll have to abandon me to my fate if we get that far.

Ben is shouting and swearing at me again. Louder this time. Imploring me to swim. I summon my last dregs of remaining energy for a final concerted effort, trying to gain more traction in the water with my arms and finally remembering to kick with my legs. We're working together now and as the river eases off a little, he's able to help me out of the main current and into calmer water. A few more strokes, some more help from Ben and I'm able to stand up and stagger over to the bank.

I suck in lungfuls of sweet Scottish air.

How do you make sense of an experience like that? Others are quick to do it for you of course, telling you to 'get back on the horse' as soon as possible. I didn't want to. I never paddled seriously again.

I did thank Ben for saving my life and made sure everyone knew what he'd done. He went on to become a policeman.

Many people will say that it was luck, pure chance that I didn't get pulled under the surface a third time, and Ben's bravery and determination that helped to get me to the side in time. And that was my conclusion for a long while…

Many years later, I'm walking across London Bridge, on my way to the office, thinking about my Autumn 100 race in a few weeks' time, and listening to the second verse of Amazing Grace on my iPhone

Through many dangers, toils and snares
I have already come
'Tis Grace that brought me safe thus far
And Grace will lead me home'

As I listen, the events on the Findhorn come flooding back, in vivid technicolour. Even though there are other commuters all around me, hurrying to work, I don't care that sudden, cathartic tears are streaming down my face. I can't help thinking that, despite my apparent unbelief at the time, I was being looked after. And on other occasions when I've been in trouble too. After all these years, I'm finally released from the trauma, and overcome by a wave of gratitude. I thank God for being alive.

3 A MAN CALLED DAVID SHARP

There's something rather sedate about running…

…Especially when you're at the back of the field at the beginning of a race, with a wall of runners in front. And even though you've started your watch already, you can only take baby steps, a well-timed stride or two.

As the seconds tick by, momentum slowly builds, and eventually, almost perfectly in synch with one other, we break into a collective jog, and carried along as a group, corner gently round past the church. There's an almost immediate anti-climax as we concertina back together, coming to an abrupt halt behind a bottleneck that's built up at the first gate. No harm done, we're soon off again, energised by a rallying call, a shout of 'HAVE A GOOD RACE!' from the nearby marshall.

There's another gate induced go-slow and then we're all walking again to negotiate a little hump-backed bridge over a stream. The first mile takes around twelve and a half minutes in the end. But soon we've finished the first section of towpath north of Streatley and out on an open track through a meadow, there's time and space for each of us to find our own rhythm.

I tell myself to ignore the throbbing sensation in my

right knee, the jolt of pain every time my right foot hits the floor. I try and take in the world around me, the competitors to the left and right, moving with an economy of effort that shows they're running within themselves.

We're in a shallow valley between the Chilterns and the Berkshire Downs and drinking in the strong autumnal sunshine, it's hard not to cast my mind back to May 2019 and my first hundred mile race along here (10). It must have been about two in the morning and I'd just stopped at an aid station inside the Morrell Room. Although I should have been exhausted I was enjoying myself, eating jelly babies out of my shorts pocket, high on the exhilaration and utter newness of racing through the middle of the night.

The watch vibrates to tell me mile two is done. Although my knee is sore and I probably won't make it very far, at least I'm getting some exercise and this is one of the most beautiful places to go trail running in the whole of England.

The only way to manage the situation is to take it one section at a time and to focus on making it to Moulsford. So I feel slightly better, when a few minutes later, we reach the first few houses, and soon we're swinging sharply left away from the river by the Beetle and Wedge pub. Here the Thames Path is routed up through the village, following the gently rising main road north to Wallingford for just under a mile.

My fitness levels are hard to get a handle on. I lost six weeks of training whilst I recovered from the slipped disc. I've done nothing for three weeks since the recce. And yet, in between I did manage to get some good miles in. I am right at the back of the field, and the pace does feel a little sedentary. Watching for oncoming cars, I swing out into the road and jog past a few people. Inevitably the knee pain ratchets up a notch or two, and chastened, I throttle back again. Soon there's some more Centurion marker tape dangling in a hedge, telling us it's time to leave the road, to veer right and follow the easy track back down towards the Thames again.

There's more pitch and roll to the path after Moulsford. It's narrower too as we negotiate banks and ditches, the odd overhanging branch alongside the river, and then have to slow up through a muddier, stickier section, where I start to wonder if I should be wearing trail shoes after all. It's over pretty soon though and I can start to think about seeing Emily in Wallingford. I told her it would be between 10 and 10.15 and checking my watch to see if I'm going to hit that window, I decide to speed up through mile six.

Just before we turn up into the town centre, there's the familiar slightly disconcerting moment when the path turns abruptly right and we're sent through a narrow tunnel in the middle of a row of terraced houses, and then we're in Wallingford.

It's 10.09am, Emily is stood on the corner of New Road, excited about being in the right place at the right time. She's followed the instructions on the Centurion website explaining where she can and can't wait and there are other supporters nearby too. We share a hug and a kiss and she asks about my knee. I tell her I can keep going for now.

10.11am, a little further up Thames Street, there are Centurion banners and trestle tables lined with food in the forecourt of Wallingford Baptist Church. I grab some banana, thoughtfully sliced into bite-sized chunks. I've told myself to forget about pacing, to go at a speed my knee can cope with, but not to hang around at the aid stations. Obviously in some kind of flow state after helping hundreds of runners, one of the volunteers has filled up my water flasks in the blink of an eye. And with his help, it's fun to treat this like a Formula One pit stop, to be in and out in about 45 seconds.

Something feels different, more expansive, as I start running again back towards the river. I give myself permission to forget about my knee. There's a sense of possibility and excitement at the potential hours of adventure ahead. I remember this emotion from the Thames and North Downs races, the sweet spot after the first stop, where you've just taken on food and water, you still have energy, your senses and concentration are in overdrive, and although it's very early on in terms of distance, you're already completely immersed in the race.

A few minutes further up the busy, beige-coloured towpath north of the town, I take stock. In the excitement of seeing Emily and nailing the aid station stop I seem to have speeded up. I've been chatting to a tall bloke with a South African accent and he's faster than me. The higher pace is helping to anaesthetise my knee but it's pushing my heart rate up into the 160s. I'm not as fit as I thought, and this is too much, time to ease off.

I'm then remembering how three years ago, in the still sub-zero darkness just before dawn, this was where it got really cold and wearing pretty much every layer from my backpack, I forced myself to run faster to warm up…

Soon we're at the end of the soft stretch of towpath and making the slightly awkward step up onto the narrow footbridge at Benson Weir. I'm distracted by the 'clank-clank' of my footfall on the metalwork and look up just in time to see a dog walker taking timely avoiding action. I throw a thank you over my shoulder and then get to glance down at the rushing water right beneath my feet.

The Thames Path performs a series of beautiful variations, twists and turns along this stretch across on the east bank. Afterwards I'll discover the full length trail was the brainchild of a man called David Sharp. He was 47 when he first outlined his vision for a continuous path from the source to the sea, but 70 by the time the National Trail was finally opened. He spent most of the second half of his life surveying, campaigning and bridge-building to

make his dream a reality (11). Clearly many other were involved, but David was the driving force.

Maybe it's inevitable that our passions take over our lives...

Up until about five years ago, ultra-marathons seemed completely out of reach from me, something for special forces types, people who were fitter and tougher. And yet now, preparing for, taking part in, and writing about them seems to be part of my DNA.

It was Dean Karnazes' immersive, 'Ultra Marathon Man' book which first piqued my interest and I tried a 50km race in May 2017 (12). Even though I got a lot of things wrong, it was clear the sport was more inclusive than I'd imagined. I graduated to a 50 mile race in May 2018, and after that, the Thames 100 miler in May 2019 (13). Journeying all day, and all through the night until daybreak, was so intense I wanted the experience again, so I did the North Downs 100 in August 2020 (14). There were some false starts due to injury in 2021, but this third 100 mile race has been at the forefront of my mind for most of 2022. Ultra-running has turned out to be highly addictive. I think there will always be 'one more race' and like David Sharp, I've found a passion for the second half of my life.

Even though I'm trying not to run too fast, I get into a nice rhythm along here on the right bank. Every now and again my Garmin watch vibrates to tell me another mile is done. And for a while I concentrate on the numbers, the satisfying task of keeping my pacing consistent – 10 minutes 14 seconds, 10:17, 10:16, 10:18…

Soon I'm weaving my way along the narrow walled section of path that zig-zags north into Shillingford and I realise it's not too much further to the turn-around point. The frontrunners will come charging through on their way back before too much longer.

There's a lot of traffic on the A4074, the main road from Reading to Oxford and we have to cross it twice. As I time my little sprint over to the other side in a break between cars, I can see Kerry, one of the other ultra-runners from Twitter trying to do the same. She's going well and heads off in front of me.

Out and back races are unusual, and in the first field along by the river, it's great to have the chance to see, up close and personal, the eye-out-on-stalks commitment of the athletes coming past at the front of the race. I don't have any delusions of grandeur, and award myself a walking break. Justified by the fact I've done 10 miles already, and I need to slow down to open and suck on a gel. In the days when I ran shorter distances, and fast times seemed everything, walking always felt like giving up, admitting failure. I'm having none of that nonsense now, and occasionally lift my head up to say well done to other runners streaming back the other way. There's dozens coming by and it can't be far to the second aid station.

Just before Little Wittenham, one of the Centurion photographers captures the moment I cross the hump-backed bridge over the river… number 258 pinned to my shorts, orange long-sleeved top pushed up to my elbows, blue ultra-vest strapped tightly across my chest. I'm staring straight into the camera, a massive toothy grin on my face, happy just to be 'in the arena', surrounded by my peers, not fussing about how fast I am.

My knee is still signalling a faint jolt of pain every time I take a stride but all the blood flow is making it more and more manageable. I won't be stopping at this checkpoint either.

About a mile into the return leg, there's an unexpected turn of events. It seems to be raining, completely unacceptable - and unforecast of course – only spitting at first, but then the intensity gradually builds until it is officially tipping it down. My initial disbelief and displeasure fade away with a little pep talk. I have to be able to cope with this sort of thing. I am a bit hot. This is actually refreshing! The mysterious shower stops as quickly as it started.

Shortly after, there are no more runners coming the other way, just the volunteer race sweeper, stalking the lady at the back of the field, arms laden with tags and marker signs.

Over the other side of the main road we've reached the point in proceedings, two and a half hours in, when even a slight uphill justifies a walking break. After a minute or two, using a slightly different set of muscles starts my knee off again and it's time to jog on.

We'll soon be back in Wallingford, where the river is wider and shallower, and in the days before bridges, there was an important ford. This is why the town grew up, and why, we're confidently told by a number of different websites, William the Conqueror crossed the Thames here on his way to London (15)…

Sorry but I do have to ask, was the great man lost? Last time I checked, you don't get from Hastings to Westminster Abbey via Wallingford!

Turns out the Norman strategist was on top of his game as ever. The only bridge across the Thames in

London was heavily fortified, so he decided to bide his time, loop round and approach the city from the north. More importantly perhaps, he wanted the Archbishop's approval for his claim to the throne, and Stigand wasn't in Canterbury when William came calling. The cleric was holed up in Wallingford and this is where William found him and persuaded him to swear allegiance to his new King (16)…

Emily's been shopping in the town. She fell in love with it during the recce weekend and loves the craft shops. This time she's found a florist. But she's dutifully stood there on Thames Street again to give me another hug as I come by, chomping on a sausage roll after the third aid station stop.

There's just over 10k left on leg one and route finding isn't going to be a problem. It's a case of finding a sustainable rhythm, the right balance between running and walking, the occasional slipstream of another runner. At the end of every field, we're holding the gates open for one another, and there's a communal rather than competitive spirit. I churn out a steady set of 11 minute miles on the way down to Moulsford and then the final stretch back to the startline.

None of the four Autumn 100 legs are exactly the right distance of course, and at 24.2 miles, this first one, is both the flattest and shortest of all. The race is only just beginning. But still, I've already made it further than I thought my knee would allow, and there's a little flurry of satisfaction as I step over the threshold into Goring Village Hall. The timing clock reads 4 hours 19 minutes and 28 seconds…

4 LONG TALL SALLY

I realise I'm going to fall off some time before it happens.

I'm bridging across an open-book corner, 30 feet up a rock climb in the Peak District and I'm stuck, unable to move up or down.

My right toe is wedged into a little pocket on the right wall, the sole of my left shoe is smeared on the gritstone wall to the left. I haven't got a decent handhold so I'm pressing my palms against the rock on both sides of the corner.

My right calf is starting to cramp up. There's nothing I can do about it. I haven't got a good enough foothold on the left wall to shift my weight onto the other leg.

Sensing the trouble I'm in, my body starts a series of physiological reactions, none of them helpful. Adrenaline floods around my bloodstream. My pulse rate and my breathing speed up. I can feel my heart thumping against the wall of my chest. My fingers and palms start to sweat profusely, making it harder to gain traction with the rock and hold my position in the corner. My best line of escape is to climb higher – after all, the top of the route, and the safe haven of the gloriously horizontal moorland, is only a few tantalising feet above me. But as panic has set in, my field of vision has narrowed, and the confidence to try another attempt at the technically difficult, friction-based move upwards, deserts me.

My right calf starts to vibrate, slowly at first and then more violently. I've been dreading this moment. Climbers call it 'disco leg' and it tends to happen when you've been stuck in the same position for too long and cramp sets in. It's exacerbated by fear.

This is why I prefer kayaking. On a river there's very little time for fear or self-doubt. When you're climbing, there's plenty of time to think.

I look down. I'm leading the climb, so the rope drops from where it's tied into my harness, 30 feet down to my belayer Matt at the base of the crag, shifting uneasily from foot to foot.

I'm a long way above my protection – the metal wedge I placed in a crack about 12-15 feet below me and clipped to the rope, to protect me in the event of a fall. The trouble is the climbing was technically difficult and I only managed to get one of these pieces in place. I should have put another one in higher up.

In a few seconds time I am going to fall off and it looks like I'm going to hit the ground…

There's something unique about the relationship you have with your climbing partner. You've probably got a similar level of ability. You'll have developed a knowledge of their strengths and weaknesses, the type of rock they prefer, how to work together on a multi-pitch route when the architecture of the crag means you can no longer hear each other's climbing calls. It's the sort of relationship it's acceptable to wax lyrical about in the pub, especially after three or four pints. In many ways you put your life in their hands…

Matt and I had climbed together a lot. We worked together as outdoor instructors at an adventure centre in Shropshire. In our spare time, which wasn't very often as we only got one day off a week, we liked going climbing. And heading off afterwards to see Norm, the landlord of the Sun Inn, for a debrief.

We'd climbed a number of multi-pitch routes together in North Wales – 'Direct Route', 'Western Slabs' and 'Nea' in the Llanberis Pass; 'Grim Wall', 'Scratch' and 'Olympic Slab' at Tremadog; 'Grooved Arete' on Tryfan (17).

You can normally tell the approximate severity of a climb from the date of the first ascent. Rock climbing didn't properly take off in the UK until around the 1890s and only really got serious when Joe Brown and Don Whillans started climbing together in the 1950s. Most of the stuff we were doing dated from the twenties and thirties, the era of the pipe-smoking ledge, gentleman climbers with tweed jackets and double-barrelled names. Nea Morin had struck a victory for equality with the climb she led (18).

British climbs have an adjectival grading system, starting with 'Easy', then 'Very Difficult' which most beginners can deal with, then running up through 'Severe', 'Very Severe', 'Hard Very Severe', and traditionally topping out with 'Extremely Severe'. The most popular of these tend to get shortened to 'VS' and 'HVS', once you've got your head round it all (19).

When Brown and Whillans led a new wave of post-war climbing the 'Extremely Severe' grade got split out into progressively harder numbers - E1, E2, E3, and up to about E8 or E9 in our day (20).

Matt and I normally did climbs in the VS category. We've come to Burbage North, a single-pitch gritstone crag near Sheffield for the first time, and I feel like I'm climbing well. I've asked to have a go at 'Long Tall Sally', which will be my first E1 lead (21) if I'm successful.

From below the route looks eminently doable – it seems like the hardest moves are in the bottom half of the climb. I've wanted to lead E1 right through my 20s and this feels like a great opportunity.

Already though, my throat is dry, my palms are sweaty and there's a nugget of doubt in my mind. I settle myself by focusing on the pre-climb preparation, the rituals that help me to concentrate and get into the right headspace for leading.

I make sure my harness is on securely, and then lay my metal 'rack' of protection onto a nearby boulder and carefully select what I need.

Onto my first right hand gear loop, karabiners facing inwards so I can get them off easily, I clip my set of nine wire 'rocks' – these are the most common form of protection for lead climbers, metal wedges ranging in size and attached to a stiff wire cord. You position them within v-shaped cracks in the rock, and if you place them correctly, they're engineered to hold you in the event of a fall.

I'm also taking with me a couple of different sized 'Friends' – camming devices that perform a similar role as protection in cracks or hollows in the rock which have parallel sides.

Finally, I attach half a dozen 'quickdraws' to the left hand gear loop on my harness – these are lengths of stitched tape with a karabiner at either end. You clip one end to your protection to extend it, and the other end to the rope, helping to hold the rope away from the rock, so it runs in a straight line down the route and doesn't drag.

I sort out our 50 metre rope at the base of the crag. I stuffed it in my sack when we finished the previous route and now feed the full length through my hands, metre by metre, to make sure it's free from tangles, so Matt doesn't have any nasty surprises when he's belaying me.

I tie a figure of eight knot about three feet along from my end of rope, then feed the end through the bottom and top loop of my harness and back around the path of the original knot to create a double figure of eight. I tie the end off with a stopper knot.

And then ritualistically, wanting to get the soles of my

rock boots as clean as possible, I meticulously wipe them on a beer towel, which we've strategically positioned at the foot of the route.

Matt attaches the rope to his belay plate about twelve feet along from me. As he calls out

'Climb when ready!'...

...he gives me a quizzical look, which seems to say 'are you sure about this?!' I grin sheepishly and call out the time-honoured reply

'Climbing!'

And then, after dipping my fingertips in the chalk bag clipped to the back of my harness, set off slowly and carefully up the route.

Bridging across the corner and finding some small but well-defined holds on the left hand wall, I find the first few moves really enjoyable. Although they're at the upper end of what I'm capable of, we've been doing routes all day and I feel tuned into the texture and friction of the rock.

There is something quite special about climbing when your mind and body are in synch – the precision of placing your toe on a tiny crease in the rock; the 3D mental chess of figuring out the next sequence; the gymnastics of contorting your body and limbs into the best position to continue; the physical demands of pulling your bodyweight vertically upwards. There have been moments of pure flow when I'm climbing. I'll always remember Scratch Arete, my first multi-pitch HVS lead, finding the wherewithal to pull through the overhang 150 feet above the Tremadog scree, and then moving up the final slab without thinking, like my mind had left my body, and I was levitating.

Gritstone has always been my favourite rock. I led Butcher Crack, a similar, technically difficult HVS (22) at the end of a long day at Stanage, a few years before and fancy that I can repeat the same feat again at a marginally harder level.

Soon I've reached the bulge halfway up the climb, and I'm able to get a good gear placement in at the back of the crack. I clip a quickdraw onto it and after asking Matt for some slack, attach this to the rope. I feel safer now and ready to try and climb through the bulge, and I manage this fairly easily using holds on the left hand wall again.

Now on the upper echelons of the climb, I struggle to get more gear in. The only placements seem to be in the crack at the back of the corner, but these are places which I need to use as hand and footholds, so I abstain. Climbing upwards I'm soon established with my right foot in the pocket near the top of the climb.

All too late I realise this is the technical crux, the hardest move on the climb, and I'm a long way above my gear. It looks as though there is a possible sequence using small creases up the left hand wall to start. The smart thing to do would be to go for it straight away. In a similar position on Butcher Crack, I'd quickly made the intuitive moves without thinking about them too much.

But now, inhibited by how poorly I've protected the route and the fact I've never led an E1 before, I pause for a crucial few seconds... And miss my moment. Once my chance has gone, it feels like it's gone for good, and I find myself increasingly stuck.

In the precise moment when I do part company from the rock, time seems to standstill. Although I'm absolutely terrified, in those first few milliseconds there's a flash of something pretty close to relief that I've given over control of the situation and I no longer have to try and figure out what to do. Whatever happens next is out of my hands. At first I'm slithering down the corner in what feels like slow motion, and I can still make out features in the rock wall opposite, individual crystals formed millions of years before, and then I start to accelerate really fast, bash hard into the bulge and I'm flipped upside down. Then there are flashes of heather, fast approaching ground and pewter-coloured sky.

Down at the bottom of the climb, Matt has an even more frightening perspective. After trying to encourage me for the last 15 minutes, he has to watch me part company from the rock, thirty feet above him, and then gather speed on the way down, eleven stone of tumbling, flailing man, coming towards him head first at 30, 40, 50 miles an hour. It is exceptionally brave then, for him to keep his wits about him, lock off the rope, and move backwards rapidly to try and take in some of the slack.

In the end, my gear stayed in place and did its job protecting me. But it was Matt who saved my life, I landed half on top of him and he held me a couple of feet above the ground. One of the pieces of gear on my harness gashed into his hand as he broke my fall.

25 years on, I say a heartfelt thank you to Matt again. And acknowledge I made a mistake. Perhaps it's easier to focus on our successes than our failures. It's hard to be honest about my pride, particularly in this instance, when it took over and clouded my judgement. But I wanted the E1 lead, the kudos, the bragging rights. I hoped it would deliver validation in some way, complete some missing part of me.

If Matt hadn't moved swiftly backwards, and held onto the rope for dear life, or if the little metal wedge I placed at the back of the bulge, had popped out with the force of the fall, I would have surely died, and probably badly injured him too.

Mum was alive back then, her breast cancer diagnosis still a few years ahead. When she found out she was rocked and chastened by what had happened and let me know this.

I now believe God was looking out for me, as well as

Matt. It's a discipline of our faith to try and be open about the times when pride gets the better of us, and lay these moments before him, so the slate can be wiped clean. I made a mistake. I should have followed my intuition as I was getting ready, but I didn't, I chose to climb on.

A few years later I will have another couple of efforts at leading E1 on the gritstone and I do make it up 'Ratline' at Birchens and 'Namenlos' at Stanage, each given E1 at the time. But both are subsequently downgraded to Hard Very Severe as opinions shifted in the following years (23). I'm left to conclude that level of skill was always just out of my reach!

5 GRIM'S DITCH

Centurion have put a one way system in place inside Goring Village Hall, the main aid station, where we get to regroup after the first leg.

Here volunteers like Stu and Spencer are putting in a mammoth shift to look after us, helping make a seemingly impossible task more bearable. We're directed in through the left hand side door, past the timing clock, and the toilets, then we double back on ourselves to go into the main room where we can get fluids, sausage rolls and such like. And after I've picked up some refreshments and head out on leg two, this circling around delivers a kind of slingshot effect, a much needed little boost of momentum to get me going again, leaving no time to think about my knee.

Back outside, there are a couple of other male runners making their way along Thames Road in my vicinity, and our little collective stays loosely together in the first few miles, walking uphill and jogging down.

This second leg, out as far as Swyncombe, will give us our first race experience of the Ridgeway, reputed to be the oldest track in Britain, a long distance route along the top of the limestone and chalk uplands exposed along a south-west-north-east orientation across the heart of England. Here neolithic travellers apparently found a drier footfall and a route that was freer from the denser woodland at valley level (24). The villages of Streatley and Goring grew up around a crucial prehistoric intersection, where the 'street' of the Ridgeway crossed the Thames.

Before we get onto higher ground, the first six miles mirror the route from leg one, up the east bank of the river, nearly as far as Wallingford, where we'll turn right and head into the Chilterns. I came to recce the route three weeks ago, so this is familiar territory, and thanks to more volunteers, there are Centurion marker tags too making our lives easier at all the junctions.

Soon we're trotting along our first section of pleasantly turfed off-road track, and several hundred tonnes of high speed train come thundering by on the embankment alongside, on their way west. The engineer Brunel built this line to connect London and Bristol and in those days it was considered cutting edge, 'God's Wonderful Railway' (25).

I manage a couple more eleven minute miles up through South Stoke and past the spot where an old ferry used to run across the river to the pub at Moulsford. Then we're onto a more rutted, pock-marked section of trail, and I have a ready-made excuse to slow down a bit. After the railway crosses overhead, there's a stretch along past a fizzing electric fence, a pleasing little interlude through the grounds of the parish church and then it's the aid station at North Stoke already.

Although the volunteers are super friendly and the atmosphere feels tight knit inside the little village hall, it seems right not to hang around. They fill my water bottles for me, I grab some watermelon and a jam sandwich, then head out again. The whole stop has only taken about 60 seconds. And after finishing the sandwich, I keep the momentum going with another eleven minute mile, jogging along a beautifully straight and spongy section of

the Ridgeway across a riverside golf course.

And then exactly six miles into the leg, there's a right angle turn and the character of the route changes completely. For the next three and a half miles we're going to follow Grim's Ditch, an ancient earthwork that runs eastwards from here.

I'd found this stretch difficult on the recce, getting back into trail running after many months on the roads. As well as some major sections uphill, even the flatter stretch of the Ditch constantly undulated up and down. To make matters worse, I was trying out a new SIS electrolyte gel and when I went to open the pack it split, spreading sticky gunk everywhere...

Anyway that was then, right now I'm jogging gently up through the first stretch of woods, cautiously crossing the very busy road and stopping to listen to the marshal positioned at the start of the narrowest section of the Ditch.

It's single track along here and he reminds me to be considerate to other people and give way when necessary. Centurion can only carry on running this event through popular countryside by looking after their relationship with locals and landowners and a lot of good PR like this, typical of their attention to detail.

A few minutes later I'm putting the marshal's instructions into action as I step aside to let the leaders of the men's race, Peter Windross and Harry Geddes, come charging through on their way back to Goring.

I'm going at a sedate pace myself, enjoying Grim's Ditch more this time and wondering why it was built. It transpires the smart money is on it forming a pre-Roman 'socio-political boundary' which marked the northern edge of a strategically significant enclosure of agricultural land. Historians have found evidence that beyond our stretch of preserved earthwork, the boundary continued across to Henley-on-Thames. The southern edge of the enclosure would then have been protected by the u-shaped loop of the river from Henley round to Wallingford (26)…

Although I'm now over 50 kilometres into my effort and taking it steady, I'm excited about seeing Emily again at Nuffield Church - about half a mile beyond the top of the Ditch. I press on up a steep climb of a couple of hundred feet, enjoying some light-hearted competition with Kerry and another lady.

Then a few minutes later, in the lane alongside Nuffield Church, Emily is stood there again in her favourite berry-coloured coat. It's lovely to see her. She's excited about being in the right place at the right time and has made friends with a few of the other supporters, waiting for their competitors to come through. Our hug causes a bit of stir. She's asking about my knee and I'm gushing and telling her it's ok but I'm slowing up and going to take about 75 minutes out to Swyncombe and back before I come by again. That's ok she tells me. She'll be there for me.

And then I'm on my own again, following a marshal's directions across the exceptionally posh hilltop golf course which seems to now take precedence over the ancient trail.

I remember the undulations of the next stretch from the recce, and after crossing another busy A-road, there's a steep downhill section twisting and turning through a wood, where it's sensible to watch out for tree roots criss-crossing the trail.

Onwards into the 'Field of Dreams', the most iconic part of the Autumn 100, where the Ridgeway crosses a massive ploughed field and the race photographer likes to capture people doing 'I'm a bird' impressions (27). I oblige obviously!

We're over 11 miles into the leg by now and I'm alongside the tall, sociable South African man again. It turns out his name is Jaco and he's doing all four 100 milers in 2022. He's calling out encouragement to people coming in the other direction on their way back, and as we negotiate the next even steeper downhill section he asks the woman coming up why she's not running?!

Soon we're striding past the Norman church and then tackling the final hill up to the checkpoint at Swyncombe. We spot an innocuous white minibus and Jaco warns me to avert my eyes:

'Don't look! It's the DNF bus!'

So that's how you get back to Goring, if you have to drop from the race. I don't want to think about it and thanks to more efficient volunteers, I'm all stocked up with food and water and on my way again in about two minutes. Jaco's still chatting but I find out later he made it to the finish ok and completed a fantastic 400 mile Grand Slam.

After a nice little jog back down the hill past the church, the next few miles of ups and downs are tough. It's nearly five o'clock by the time I trudge back across the golf course and reach Emily again.

It's going to be too late for her to come and see me on leg three so she gives me a pep talk, telling me I'm going to make it. I tell her I'll go gently on my knee and be happy if I finish, even if it's 27 hours and 59 minutes and I'm in last place.

She gives me a final hug, we say our goodbyes, and then I'm turning left off the road and jogging gently along the top of the field, picking my way judiciously across dried mud and taking time to admire the far-reaching views to the north. Soon I'm trundling into the woods and heading more steeply down towards the top of Grim's Ditch. And then back on the Ditch itself, gently speeding up with the increasing gradient…

Beech trees are casting shadows across the trail. The afternoon sun is low in the sky, flashing and flickering through gaps in the trees, landing hot and intense on the back of my retina - like a recovered home movie of childhood, the summer of 76 and all that.

I'm completely alone in what feels like a wilderness. My heartrate has been up above 150 for hours and now here in the woods, I find much-needed calmness, a compelling conviction I don't have to strive any more, that having the courage to start, to be given the opportunity to finish, that will be enough for me.

I'm overcome with a sense of peace. It feels like God is nearby. I have Emily. I have my faith back. There is nothing for me to prove.

…And then, down in a little dip, I'm not alone any more. Brian is stood at the top of the ditch, coming the other way, hanging in there on his uphill leg, still in the race.

He's wearing an infectious Cheshire cat grin, a this-is-stupid, let's-not-take-ourselves-too-seriously sort of grin. It is lovely to see him. I'm not sure what emotion this is but it must be very close to joy. Don't start crying, it would be embarrassing. The two of us, last seen together writing ourselves off at the back of the pack at the start, feel like it's appropriate to hug.

Down at the bottom of the hill, back on the narrow single-track section, the moment of quiet has passed and I seem tangled up, trying to overtake or be overtaken by other runners. I slow down and count to ten, resisting the temptation to get pulled along in the rush.

Eventually I'm down by the river again.

I'm on mile 43, eight and three quarter hours in, and feeling it, having to resort to my old trick of counting every second right step to prolong a running effort.

'One, step, step, step,
two, step, step, step,
three…'

I tell myself I need to make it to 30, before I stop and walk again. Soon I'm back on the lovely section of straight sloping track down into North Stoke.

There's a familiar looking face from Twitter inside the village hall

'You're Keith aren't you?'
'Well done! I can barely remember my own name at 40 miles let alone someone else's!'

The sun has set, and it's hard to see through the gloom as I make my way up tree-covered Ferry Lane into the little hamlet of South Stoke. I want to try and make it back to Goring before the light goes completely and I have to put my headtorch on. I know from my instructing days that night vision works best in gradually fading light and it feels like I'm rolling back the years to use it again.

Even though I haven't been racing for ages, it's about twenty to seven now and I suddenly switch on to the fact there's still an outside chance of completing leg two inside 10 hours. I find another gear and manage some longer spells of running, breaking into a sprint on the final straight along Thames Road.

The timing clock reads 9 hours 56 minutes and 33 seconds as I stumble breathlessly back into Goring Village

Hall.

//TW

Trigger warning regarding Chapter 6.

Even though young people's mental health has been hit hard by the pandemic, it's still something that many families find hard to talk about. So it feels right to finally be open about, and share, a mental health crisis I had at the age of 20, and what helped me through it. The process of writing it down has been cathartic, but I want to flag that the content includes a self-harming incident, and for some people it may trigger thoughts or feelings that aren't easy to deal with.

Help is available via www.samaritans.org or their helpline 116 123 which is open 24 hours a day, 365 days a year. Young people can access help via www.youngminds.org.uk/young-person/find-help/

6 'YOU CAN'T SLEEP HERE!'

A lot of people seem to be upset...

The chaplain is at a loss to understand why I would do that to myself. He tells me I have plenty of friends, there are others in college who would give anything for a set of mates like mine.

Dad is fearful future employers might notice the scars and I'll have trouble getting a job. As we go for a pick up the pieces walk round Rutland Water, he suggests we start thinking about plastic surgery to cover them up, so nobody notices.

Mum is troubled when she goes to change the dressings on my wrists, working with the kind of tenderness you might expect from a professional nurse looking after her youngest son. She wonders why I'm only talking to Heather about it, why I'm not telling her what's wrong.

The Doctor at Addenbrookes is irritated when I show up in casualty for the second time in three days, presenting with the same issue. She explains I've left her with no choice, she's sending me to Fulbourn this time. I'm being sectioned, and it almost seems like a punishment. A young nurse in the taxi plays good cop, telling me it's probably for the best, only a precautionary thing…

Ten days earlier it had all been very different, a committed little group of us watching the news every evening, glued to the boxy late-eighties television at the back of a darkened room next to the JCR, John Simpson the man of the moment, in his element, bringing us nightly updates from the fast moving events in East Germany (28). And on November 9th 1989, when the wall is finally opened, and people began to flood through the checkpoints, we want to be in on the action.

'The Berlin Seven' is swiftly formed. A group of up-for-it, first and second year Corpus undergrads, marching across the market square in Cambridge, looking to put our plan into effect…

But in those days, with the internet still a few years away, and EasyJet not yet invented, you couldn't just get across Europe at the drop of a hat. Sat in the travel agent chatting to the lady bringing up options on her monitor, it becomes obvious the journey isn't going to be easy. All she can organise on our behalf is a coach to Heathrow, followed by a flight to Frankfurt and then the overnight train to Berlin. And this will cost hundreds of pounds none of us have actually got. The group rapidly dwindles in size and soon there's only two of us left. I fancy myself as a bit of a rebel – missing lectures on a regular basis, roof climbing around New Court and smoking floppy pack Marlboro Reds. NatWest have given me a £2,000 overdraft, I can get the money and I want an adventure. Tim is up for it too…

In the end Berlin and the wall itself are a bit of anti-climax. The overnight train from Frankfurt is exciting enough, especially when we enter into East Germany and we're cross examined by a pair of border guards straight out of a Cold War spy movie. But when we get to the city itself, the air is bitterly, bone-chillingly cold - the sort of deep-in-the-heart-of-the-European-continent cold I haven't experienced before and am in no way ready for. And in the travel agents, flushed with our powerful visionary idea, and self-importance, Tim and I hadn't bothered with some of the more trivial details, like organising a place to sleep.

There is still that prized photo kicking around somewhere in a box in the attic. I had a mop of mousy-coloured hair in those days, a grey fleece that was woefully inadequate for the cold, and typically unfashionable, too-big-for-my-face eighties glasses. I'm wearing a cheeky grin as I chip chunks of cement out of the wall with a tiny hammer…

On the second night, as we try and bed down in our sleeping bags in the Zoologischer Garten underground, the local West German police are having none of it, have had enough of chancers like us travelling across Europe to join the party. My German improves as Tim explains why they keep saying

'Du kannst nicht hier schlafen!'

By the third night without any sleep, traveling back on the train to Frankfurt, we're both utterly wrecked and desperate to get home. And there's still the flight and the coach journey to go.

After, in the November dark, alone in my room on the top floor of my college digs at the end of Trumpington Street, I feel numb, very small indeed. I can't stop playing the latest Enya album on my Walkman and I feel like I'm being carried away by the music, detached from my body, freefalling, and unable to control powerful negative thoughts.

Making it to Berlin and back had been a powerful statement of intent, an act of self-expression almost. But now it seems meaningless. People are going about their lives completely disinterested. I'm hopelessly behind with my degree, completely broke, and more tired than I've ever been in my life. To make matters worse the girl I was interested in has let it be known that we're only going to be 'just friends'.

I think it's the come down after such a powerful experience that I find hardest to deal with. There are a lot of parallels with my trip to K2 Base Camp the year before. I'd found the 200 mile trek in Northern Pakistan very demanding and I'd been ill on a lot of the days, losing three stone in the process. Both times I'd given my all, investing everything physically, mentally and spiritually into the adventure. Both times I think I expected a special homecoming, some form of recognition or validation, praise even. Both times I had no sense of what the plan would be afterwards. Years later, I'll figure out a solution for this kind of scenario – write a book about it. But back then, for that raw 20 year old, such self-awareness, a hard-won method of processing the experience, was nowhere to be seen. Nor was God either apparently…

In my teenage years, I'd been a strong Christian, converted with help from a couple of evangelical youth workers who ran the local 'Crusaders' group in the village where we grew up. Peter and Sonya gave up their free time to teach us, take us to the ice rink and to football tournaments, look after us on weekend residentials.

When a lady from America came to visit, she lay her hands over my head and started praying in tongues. I was overcome by an incredible groundswell of love and joy, and I cried a lot of happy tears. She even prophesied that I 'would become a great intercessor'. Unfortunately my beliefs weren't rooted enough to survive contact with studying Religious Studies at A Level and Theology for my degree. The textbooks and scholars were telling me the bible wasn't all true, that passages like the nativity story weren't actually based on historical events. So I'd ended up turning away from God disappointed, and he was the last thing on my mind as my mental health deteriorated after Berlin.

In the end, a couple of days apart, there are the two self-harming incidents, when I inflict damage to my wrists. There is a lot of blood and mess and confusion, especially the second time. And on both occasions, at least I have the wherewithal, enough desire, to stay alive and seek help.

There's then shame and embarrassment, and a traumatising spell in the Fulbourn 'mental hospital' (as they were known in those days). One of the psychiatrists wakes me up at four or five in the morning, just as I've finally fallen into a deep sleep. He marches me into a cold laboratory where I'm interviewed and grilled about my reasons for doing it. Apparently I was more likely to spill the beans when woken up abruptly. It is with some relief that I eventually figure out that, even if the doctors advise against it, I am legally allowed to discharge myself. I head back into town to face the music.

I didn't feel like I deserved it, but in the aftermath as well as those who were upset, there were lots of people who showed me kindness. Sometimes the two groups overlapped of course…

The Senior Tutor tells my Mum and Dad he thinks I'm more grown up than a lot of people in my year group, helps me to clean up the mess in my room, and finds me nicer digs, closer to college.

Mum and Dad take me to a hotel in Borrowdale for Christmas.

My brother-in-law Jon gets us tickets to watch the Test Match at Trent Bridge and Mark Ramprakash says thank you as I throw the ball back to him in the nets.

My friend Charlie Mount buys me a three-cassette recording of Handel's Messiah for Christmas. It comes in a posh box.

My sister Heather gives me emotional first aid, listening and empathising, hanging out with me without trying too hard, making it clear that she understands and she doesn't think it's my fault.

And finally, as will often be the case in the future, physical activity helps me find a way through the worst of it and out the other side.

Incidentally this is one of the reasons I've made the decision to donate the proceeds from these books to support London Youth. In the aftermath of the pandemic, their team are trying to give as many young people as possible access to free sport, not least because of its redemptive power, the positive impact it can have on mental as well as physical health.

Anyway I digress, back in Spring 1990 I'm given the opportunity to sit in the stroke seat, to be the person who sets the pace, for the newly formed Corpus Christi Men's Third Eight. Charlie goes behind me at seven.

Although the boat is mainly made up of beginners, and we don't take ourselves too seriously, we gel together as a group and perform strongly in the Lent Bumps. There's a moment when we're just about to be caught by an eight made up of rugby players - complete with a rubber duck on the bow of their boat. Our pride is triggered and we pull clear with a surge I've instigated at stroke, a don't-mess-with-us vengeance. We row very powerfully away as a unit, and it feels amazing, rocket-fuelled.

Most of us are promoted to the Second Boat in the May Bumps, me still at stroke, and we manage to catch the boat ahead of us on all four days, winning a coveted set of blades.

And later in 1990, almost exactly 12 months after being admitted to Fulbourn, even though I'm still scrawny after Pakistan and, unlike those around me, didn't row at school, I make it into the coveted position of Stroke of the Corpus Christi College Men's First Eight for the

Cambridge Winter Head Race…

7 NIGHT FLIGHT

I'm in another race, this time 100 miles on foot…

A little group of us head west, retracing the journey we made to the startline ten and a quarter hours earlier, over the twin bridges, and up Streatley High Street - straight past the Thames Path fingerpost this time.

At the end of leg two, flushed with satisfaction from running in just under the ten hour mark, I'd awarded myself the luxury of a fifteen minute stop inside the village hall - the chance to change into a warmer top, dig out a fresh pair of socks, and enjoy a warm cup of chicken soup, which Stu had kindly gone to fetch for me. As ever it was hard to leave the warm, the festivities - Spencer was there too - but needs must. Back out in the race, here in the Saturday evening dark, there's the small matter of the next 25 miles to take on. There's no talking now. It's quite serious all of a sudden and the competitors in my vicinity have a distinct 'going-for-a-ONE-DAY-buckle' vibe.

As we climb just over 100 feet in the first mile, they all seem to be walking incredibly fast. I allow the purposeful figure ahead to pull me along for a while, turning right at the top of the high street, and then sticking to the narrow pavement at the side of the main A329 road heading off to

Wallingford. As the road narrows, and the cars come flooding by only a few feet away, I pass the entrance to Townsend Farm, the place where Emily and I stayed during the recce weekend. And then, waiting for a gap in the traffic, we fork left onto the Wantage road. A minute or two later we go left again, this time onto the quieter Rectory Road, out-of-town now, heading up towards the golf course. I'm glad I've checked this stretch out already and don't have to worry about route finding.

Eventually there's a respite from striding uphill and I can put in a jogging effort, albeit only temporarily. The watch vibrates to tell me that's the 50 mile mark and I engage in a back and forth tussle with a couple of committed-looking guys for a quarter of a mile or so. Then they seem to find another gear and forge ahead, leaving me alone in the dark, striding up the little lane towards the trailhead where the Ridgeway proper starts.

Here, about two and a half miles into the leg, there's a more significant climb, and suddenly one after another, a couple of the leaders of the race come haring down towards me, 20 miles further on, headtorch beams jagging around in the dark, arms flailing around as they try to negotiate their almost out of control descent.

Dismiss the demoralising thought that it will be six or seven hours before you're doing the same. Concentrate on your own effort. Forget about them. You've done this before. The outward leg has three main sections, four miles uphill, two miles down, and then six up again. Let's get the first bit of up ticked off.

Just over fifteen minutes later, a couple of hundred feet higher, I'm on the top of the Berkshire Downs, and shivering with cold, as a gusty westerly wind makes itself known for the first time. James did warn us and this buffeting in-your-face breeze won't be letting up until the turnaround at Chain Hill, nine miles ahead.

A few more minutes and I'm picking my way downhill on the chalky rutted trail, keeping my eyes open for an easy-to-miss fork left. I don't have anything to worry about. As ever there's the Centurion marker tag, luminous in the beam of my headtorch, twirling around in the breeze. There's a slightly built woman hereabouts, lifting her feet up like a ballerina as she runs down the rutted slot on the left hand side of the track. My effort to overtake her pushes my heart rate up and she comes past me walking up the next little rise.

All too soon I'm at the bottom of the downhill stretch and walking, occasionally jogging, along a little lane, the flattish stretch before the main climb. When I ran this leg on the Sunday morning three weeks before, this was where my knee began to twinge with pain and I tried to dismiss it, thinking running another 21 miles on it would be ok!

About that knee - right now eleven hours into the race, it does seem to be properly numb, not bothering me enough to be an issue, like God has actually answered my prayer. I'm not going to flog it to death though and that's probably why the little posse of sub-24 hour strivers have left me behind…

I push on up the first hill and soon sense activity up ahead. There's something of a party atmosphere at East Ilsley aid station, fairy lights, music and a crew of jolly volunteers, pleased to have another runner to look after, something to do in the cold. I thank them, and celebrate by chomping down a couple of slices of watermelon and a jam sandwich that's a bit too chilly and sets my teeth on edge. I stuff another one into the pocket of my shorts, and get gunk on my hands as I try to close the zip.

Heading off again, making my way up the paved road alongside a set of gallops, it dawns on me I've made a fairly big mistake. All this time, I've been giving myself a pat on the back for my efficiency at aid stations, born out of experience apparently. But in my enthusiasm, I seem to have shot out of Goring Village Hall without my walking pole. That wasn't part of the plan. As expected I'm not running very much anymore and it would have helped along here, would have taken the load off my legs. Hmmm... maybe you're not so smart as you think...

Traffic noise starts to be discernible alongside the wind, as we head up towards the A34, the main road north round here. I find myself head-to-head with another guy. After we've kept each other honest for a few minutes, I tell him he's going well and he pushes on, leaving me alone again with a second rather crumpled sandwich.

A few minutes later, the path veers right, swinging down beneath the busy road, and someone is shining a light in my eyes from the far end of the underpass. It's all a bit sci-fi for my liking and, after being in the dark for so long, his torch is UFO bright, almost blinding. I instinctively slow up, sensing danger. But it's ok, turns out he's a race photographer, warning me to contour round to the left as I go by, to avoid a muddy quagmire. I mutter a thank you and dig in for the steep pull back up to ground level and the main track.

I should be running more. It's less than a mile from the A34 to the first car park and this seems to be taking forever. My bamboo running top is really warm but it is only one layer and constantly heading into this seemingly gale force wind, little by little, I'm getting progressively colder.

About twenty to ten, on the steeper pull up to the second car park, I'm thinking of Emily tucked up in the warm in the B&B and sufficiently weary to allow myself a pick me up – I ring her up to say night night and then listen to an unexpected story about wet coal and the fire in the living room smoking out the house.

Talking to Emily helps me to switch on, think about race management. I get my act together, finally doing something about the fact the windchill has got into my bones. In the welcome shelter of a little clump of trees, I stop to put my jacket on. It's hard work getting the pack off my back. My shoulder and back muscles have been held in the same position for hours and object to being

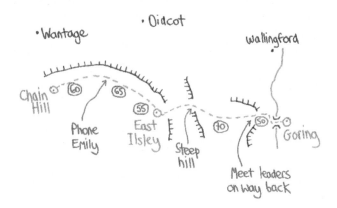

pulled in different directions. Dazed from 58 miles of effort, it takes me a bit of time to awkwardly peel the pack off, drop it to the ground and fumble around to open the back compartment zip with my cold hands. It's a relief to slide the extra layer on.

I know from the recce it's still 2.7 miles to the turnaround at Chain Hill and the next stretch drags. Emily's probably going to be drifting off to sleep sometime soon. Normally I would be too. I've stiffened up after the stop and it's really hard to motivate myself to dig in for even a short running effort. I'm stuck on 16 minute miles and the cluster of sub-24 runners are long gone up ahead. It's just me and the night sky, and my God… Time to be thankful for being alive, for still being in the race, for my somehow anaesthetised knee.

Eventually I get to the final turn up to Chain Hill, the place where Jon Jones explained in his blog how he'd gone straight on during last year's race (29). Easily done of course, the camber of the main track takes you obviously downhill and it seems counter-intuitive to strike left. He quickly rectified his mistake and went on to a sub-23 hour finish - that sort of heroism seems significantly out of reach as I plod slowly up the hill to the monument.

Actually its Lord Wantage Monument to you! The obelisk was established in memory of Robert Loyd-Lindsay, the military man and member of the landed gentry who'd helped set up the British Red Cross – as a brief google had revealed after I'd done the recce (30)…

It's a clear night, and the pillar is clearly visible to my left, meaning there's only just under half a mile to go. We had it easy on legs one and two, just over 48 miles in total, and now we seem to making up the difference…

Thirteen and a half hours into the race, up here on top of the Ridgeway, the aid station feels like an outpost on the far side of the moon. Inside the buffeted little marquee, there's shelter from the wind at least. And committed and welcoming volunteers filling my water bottle. One directs me towards the jelly babies, while another gently tells the man slumped in a camping chair with his head in his hands that perhaps he might be better off getting up and carrying on. I know I need to too. It would be very easy to procrastinate and start royally faffing about. But if I'm more than 90 seconds or so, I'll get cold, stiffen up dramatically and be even slower on the way back…

It feels lonely out in the dark again and it takes time to warm up.

Mid way through mile 62 I recognise the slumped over man, back on his feet again and coming past me. I shout across a respectful 'well done' for getting up again.

And now there's only me. And Orion's Belt of course, askew in the eastern sky, sat at an unfamiliar angle, a tangerine-coloured moon alongside. It looks like a stage backdrop, pinned there for my benefit, just above Goring at the end of the leg. Never getting any nearer. Gary Tuttle named the boy they lost Orion (31). Somewhere ahead of me he must have seen these stars too…

There's always the wind, the howling and buffeting wind. It's swirling around from behind me now at least, occasionally giving me a helpful nudge in the back.

It feels like I'm on a night flight, a window seat traveller taking in the sleeping world below. To the north and north-east, there are smudged clusters of light in the middle and far distance, Wantage, Didcot, and other settlements hunkered down for the night.

Up here there's an irregular procession of headtorches coming my way. Competitors still trudging out to Chain Hill in threes and fours and fives. The lights look far away but all too soon, they're blinding me and I'm doing a polite, give way detour, ceding my little section of track to offer them right of way. One of them might have just shouted 'Hello Gareth!'... or did I imagine it amidst this blustery wind?

I'm craving, craning for the outline of the clump of trees by the second car park, which will mean I've made a bit of progress on the way back.

This slow pace is such a contrast to when I was here three weeks ago on the recce, buoyed up by meeting Emily in the car at Chain Hill, three mini sausage rolls, and the prospect of back-to-back marathons; happily cantering along at an I-can-run-for-ever sub 10 minute mile pace, arms out on the downhill sections for balance, skipping past the little groups of ramblers and picnickers, shouting out hello. And with all that adrenaline, running the second half of the leg faster than the first. Slower than 2020 of course, I'll always be slower than 2020, but feeling like I'd got some form.

Now I'm merely mid-trudge. And yet. It's me and my Maker. How many more times in my lifetime will I be out in the wilds, awake and on the move after lights out, taking encouragement from the solitude, the watching moon, the gentle voice in my head telling me I'm doing ok, I'm still in the race.

Miles blur together. I lose track of time. It must be nearly midnight now. Someone's moved all the landmarks further apart.

Eventually I am jogging down by the gallops, imagining a baddie from a Dick Francis novel might jump out on me

(32), tackling the final stretch of track before East Ilsley. Back at the mid-leg aid station, even the volunteers are cold. Wrapped up in coats and hats, two of the ladies are swinging their arms back and forth to stay warm. I need to too, and won't if I stick around here too long. By my calculations it could still take nearly two hours to get back to Goring.

A cup of Coke and I'm off again, turning left, pulling over the little crest, and forcing myself to jog for a couple of minutes down the last section of hill.

Before I did my first hundred mile race I was worried about keeping awake through the night. When it comes down to it, this doesn't ever seem to be much of a problem, your body has enough adrenaline going round to stop you falling asleep. But it's a weird feeling, pushing on after midnight having covered nearly 70 miles. I'm light-headed and disorientated, thirsty, frustrated that when my brain tells my legs to move there now seems to be a timelag. Even though I miss my stick, there's nothing left to do but push on up the hill, accept this is going to be an 18 minute mile and hope it comes to an end eventually.

It's a relief to get to the top and start heading down the last stretch of the Ridgeway track to the roadhead. This is where I went charging past a group of charity runners on the recce, exhilarated at finding form, pushing for a sub four and a half hour trail marathon. But now, even though it's steeply downhill I feel wasted and can only manage a short spell of running.

It's just before two in the morning as I eventually make my way through a deserted Streatley, across the two bridges and in through the back door of the village hall for the third time, with the race clock reading 16 hours 53 minutes and 12 seconds. Leg three has taken a long time. I don't care, it just feels good to be back in the warm.

8 EMILY

The South Downs 100 miler is a week away and I'm in the form of my life.

It's the last Saturday in October 2020 and this time I've got the preparation right, managing to run 50 miles back-to-back a few weeks out from the race and stay injury free. If everything goes to plan, a sub-24 hour 'ONE DAY' buckle is definitely in play, despite all the hills.

All my kit is ready for the race and laid out in the front room. Disposable cup, backpack, poles, beanie, gloves, headtorch, spare headtorch, space blanket, South Downs Way map, whistle...and the number 78 with GARETH written in red along the bottom. Everything is in place.

What was that psychological advice my friend Paolo had given me? Don't put all your eggs in one basket, don't invest your whole personality in a single pastime. You've got too much to lose if the worst happens.

Too late... There's another Covid news conference. Cases have been rising for weeks now, and even though he's been prevaricating, even though it takes him over four minutes of rambling to get to the point (33), Boris Johnson finally tells everyone...

'YOU MUST STAY AT HOME'

...effective from Thursday 5th November, an agonising 48 hours out from the race.

James from Centurion emails the day after to confirm the race is cancelled.

Even though this is clearly the right thing to do from a public health point of view, it still feels to me like the sky has fallen in. To make matters worse I pick up an Achilles injury and can't even go running. My mental health nosedives. I'm home alone, still coming to terms with my relationship ending after 13 years and Novembers are hard at the best of times. This isn't the best of times.

I don't look after myself very well, indulging in a set of behaviours that don't do me any favours. I'm being sucked into a tailspin, freefalling, in a similar state of disorientation to the aftermath of Berlin.

Eventually November comes to an end and the sun still comes up every morning.

In early December, at the same time as some of the restrictions are lifted, I have an online session with Steve Dewar, a coach and counsellor who's been helping me all year. He knows how much running means to me and listens while I pour out my feelings. We get talking about negative capability, coping with uncertainty. He reminds me how I managed to do this in the North Downs race. Steve then gets onto one of his favourite topics – the liminal zone - how during major life events, of course we have to leave a lot of things behind, but, as we search for a new direction, when we're in the space where we feel most lost, if we remain open to possibility, that in-between place where it feels like there's no sight of land, can actually contain great power and creativity.

So I'm in a different frame of mind for a Zoom party on Friday 11th December to say goodbye to Jas Hothi, one of London Youth's longest serving members of staff. And I'm intrigued and excited when my colleague Zoë introduces her seemingly shy friend and housemate Emily, a few drinks into the call.

A week of introductory texting follows. Emily and I arrange to meet in-person the Saturday after. As I drive to meet her for the first time, excited about our date, the heavens open and there's a torrential downpour, accompanied by the most intense 3D rainbow I've ever seen. I'm driving through the centre of it, vibrant colours everywhere and the sun reflecting off the road turns thousands of raindrops to gold in the translucent light.

The date goes well, she is gorgeous, and we go for a walk round a muddy Hainault Forest, clicking immediately and holding hands before we're back at the car park. The next day Emily and I hang out together too. On the way back from another walk, I'm drawn to an advert on the side of a passing double decker bus…

'Come to me, all you who are weary and burdened, and I will give you rest.'
Matthew 11.28

After running 6,500 miles in the last three years – pushing myself to train again and again and again, after a tumultuous 12 months of Covid, after a horrible November, the words cut through. It feels like Emily is a gift, a respite from the storm. She's an accomplished violinist and pianist and a few days later she plays me Bach's Prelude in C Major. It is soft and hypnotic and deeply moving. I can't stop the tears rolling down my face.

We formed a household support bubble as the restrictions ratcheted up again, and in the first half of 2021 we get to know each other more and start planning a future together. Inspired by Emily's own Christian faith and the words on the side of the bus, I turn back towards God for the first time in over three decades. And although I'm yet to become a Christian again, I am once more open to the possibility that Jesus might be God's son, that he might have died to save me, and others who are lost like me.

Unable to go to church in person, Emily tunes into the online services from Soul Survivor (34), a church she'd previously been to near Watford. I start watching them with her. For thirty years I've had a distrust of evangelical preachers, my default position to tune them out, dismiss them as too dogmatic to make time for. But there's something about Mike Pilavachi I warm to. He has a dry sense of humour, and although he doesn't take himself too seriously, he takes his faith seriously and talks a lot of sense.

One week Mike is raving about a book that's made a deep impression on him - 'Gentle and Lowly' by Dane Ortlund (35). He's does a good job of selling it and when Emily buys it, I'm intrigued and start reading it myself. I'm still not a Christian though, just an interested agnostic.

It turns out the title is taken from Matthew 11.29, the next verse on from the one I saw on the side of the bus

'Take my yoke upon you, for I am gentle and lowly at heart.'

The book focuses on the character of Christ and in particular his unfiltered heart, the way he feels deeply for, and is immediately drawn towards, and drawn to heal, those who are suffering.

I'm inspired to read John's Gospel for the first time. I'd always steered away from it before but I find it compelling. It's powerful and poetic, packed full of social justice, reading like an eyewitness account, as a radical Jesus demonstrates he's the son of God through a series of signs and miracles. The first two are counter-intuitive. At a wedding in Cana, when the guests run out of alcohol, he turns 600 litres of water into wine. Then he approaches a Samarian woman at a well, and reveals himself as the Messiah to her, even though she's someone he wouldn't normally have talked to in the culture of the time.

He sets off around the Judean countryside full of compassion and goodness, healing an official's son, a man who hadn't walked for 38 years, a man born blind. He walks on water, feeds 5,000 people. When the crowd following him asks how they should respond, Jesus tells them to believe in him…

'…whoever comes to me will never go hungry… will never be thirsty…'

I read a series of books by Mike Pilavachi and his Soul Survivor colleague Andy Croft. They bring John and other biblical characters like Elijah and Joseph to life (36).

When the restrictions lift, Emily and I start going to St. Mary's Church in Chigwell. The church is welcoming, the teaching uncomplicated and it feels nice to be part of a congregation.

I don't have a sudden revelation, a conversion experience. My journey to recovering my Christian faith happens almost imperceptibly, Emily alongside. It's rather like the way night becomes day, a very faint softening at first, some colour appearing, and then gradually as the sun climbs towards and above the horizon you become aware it's fully light.

One day, Emily and I are back in Hainault Forest again, this time with her brother Neill. He's a well-built man who can obviously take care of himself, streetwise, used to do a lot of boxing. He is a Christian too and as we're walking I am overcome by an overpowering feeling of love for him, combined with a surge of joy, a recognition of his redemptive qualities. Hiding tears, I ask him if I can give him a hug. It feels like the Holy Spirit is close at hand.

I hear a sermon on the Parable of the Prodigal Son (37) and this time the story holds a powerful personal meaning.

The son turns away from his father and squanders his inheritance in a distant country. He spends years in a faraway place become more and more lost. Eventually he decides to head back. On his way home, his father sees him from a long way off, and runs to meet and embrace him full of joy. I've turned away from God for so long, 32 or 33 years, and it feels amazing that he waited for me, that he's welcoming me back with open arms…

It's Sunday 9th May 2021, and we're in the garden of Emily's house in Chigwell, celebrating our birthdays, and she's wearing her pretty blue dress and cardigan. There's a select gathering of seven of us, the maximum permitted by the new regulations. A big dark rain cloud is approaching which will break the party up soon, as the guests aren't allowed indoors as well. It's now or never. I bend down on one knee and look into her eyes

'I love you, you make me happy. I want to make you happy. Will you marry me?'

She says yes!

9 WELCOME TO READING

There are two marshals on patrol, standing outside the Village Hall, braving the middle of the night cold. I say my goodbyes, telling them I may be some time…

To kick off leg four, the route heads down through Goring Gap, the narrow valley between the Chilterns and the Berkshire Downs, an important landmark for geography enthusiasts. When the Thames pooled into a giant lake during the ice age, this is the place where the water overflowed through a weakness in the escarpment, forging a new path south (38)…

Once I'm out beyond the last lights of the town, back in the dark of the night, the river seems otherworldly, an expanse of black revealed in the pool of my headtorch, only a few feet away on the right. It would be very easy to trip on a tree root and fall in. I'm tired and need to take care. At least the path is sheltered by the surrounding hills, and after all that wind on top of the Downs, there is an intense, almost blissful silence. It reminds me of the kind of quiet you get when you put your head on the pillow after a night out.

There were saucepans full of hot cheese and tomato pasta at the Village Hall. Stu fetched me a much needed helping. I remembered my walking pole this time…

My little reverie is broken by sudden drama, a flurry of activity, the front of the women's race. Here comes Debbie Martin-Consani in first place, going so well it looks like her pacer is struggling to keep up. And then ten minutes of plodding later, here is Ally Whitlock too, no longer in the middle of the pack, charging back to Goring on her way to a career-best second place (39).

The path heads away from the river and it's time for me to tackle the steep section up into the woods. This hill is etched in my memory, I remember running down it full of excitement, going well in the Thames 100 (40). It feels weird tackling it from the other direction, pushing down on my thighs as I march upwards trying to stick to some sort of respectable pace.

What with the climb coming so early in the leg, it's difficult to get any momentum going, and do much running. And once I've crossed the toll bridge over the Thames, still operational in 2022, I shouldn't be stopping again at Pangbourne aid station just over four miles in. But I need the toilet, and find myself heading in. Upstairs in the warm, some genius has provided little pots of custard. While I scoff one, I eavesdrop on the third lady, Mari Mauland, having a relaxed conversation with a volunteer about the difficulty of taking on food during the super-hot Western States 100 mile race in California.

Back outside, it feels significantly colder and while I'm dawdling along the first meadow by the river, seventy-something Centurion-stalwart Ken Fancett comes past me. He's famously good at pacing so it's almost a privilege - almost but not quite! He keeps me honest and I speed up trailing in his wake through mile 81.

A mile or two later there's another detour away from the river, uphill again. I just have to suck it up and go at a sustainable I guess.

Heading into the hamlet of Purley on Thames, I take care to open and close the metal gate gently. It's about

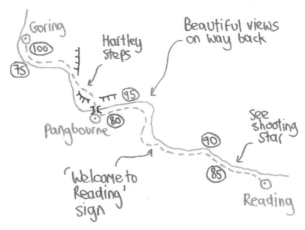

twenty past four in the morning and it seems right to try and muffle the clang, to be 'aware of the residents' - as the Centurion sign suggests. I'm conscious too of the click-clack of my walking pole on the pavement and try not to be too noisy with it.

There's a confusing section through a little estate - it would be easy to get lost without the Centurion marker tape, and then after a gentle drag up through a little wood I reach the 'Welcome to Reading' sign, infamous in ultra-running circles as you're not in Reading, not by any stretch of the imagination, and the aid station is still a long way off. I'm not going to fall into this mental trap I tell myself, I've been here before, I know it all…

I head over the main line railway and down the Tilehurst station steps where the Thames Path rejoins the towpath along by the river. A little further on I'm in catching distance of my first Autumn 100 competitor for a while. He has a pacer (permitted in this final leg) and they seem to be engaged in a fairly colourful discussion. The pacer seems to be under the impression that a sub-24 hour time is still on the cards and wants to press on, the runner is struggling to keep up and coughing and retching with the effort. I know who's side I'm on!

This pair seem to be in close proximity for mile after mile, and with my pace dropping to 16, 17 minute miles at the back end of the night, this stretch seems to drag on and on. The lights of Reading town centre are some way ahead even now, and once I get there it's still a long way to the aid station at the far end. In my sleep deprived stupor, self-doubt starts to flood round my tired head. Even though I ran the other way in the Thames 100 I haven't done a recce along here, and I'm not sure how far it is to the turnaround. The first two legs were short, so it could be further than I'm expecting. What if I slow up even more? I'm struggling with worst case scenario calculations, might death march 25 minute mile pace result in me failing to finish inside 28 hours? I slip into a dark place, low on blood sugar, resentful at how long this is taking, wondering when this outward leg will ever end…

There's a tangible and intense stillness just before dawn. The river holds its breath. The swans and geese are still asleep. The other birds seem to sense something. Self-doubt has been a thorn in my side for an hour now. And then as I lift my head to the heavens for inspiration, it feels like God is on my side again, as a shooting star skids down across the sky. Although it's only fleeting, the sense of reassurance, the feeling I'm going to be ok, comes flooding back.

We press on through the town centre, past Caversham Lock, work our way across Kings Meadow, climb wearily up and down the bridge over the River Kennet. Even then it's still another half a mile.

In the end, about five miles on from the 'Welcome to Reading' sign, the lights of Wokingham Waterside Centre are the most beautiful sight in the world. A kindly volunteer, sleep-deprived herself, takes pity on me and fetches me a hot chocolate. There's the opportunity to gently explain to pacer guy why a sub-24 hour time has long since passed his runner by, but he still seems unconvinced.

61

It's time to set off again, try and retrace my steps back to Goring. Ahead of me my two companions are deep in conversation. Or at least one of them is. The runner is using all is breath to keep up. A man in one of the houseboats moored along the bank has his light on, obviously through with being disturbed…

I get a flashback to one of the times I did the 100 Mile Canoe Test with London Youth, our group of young people from a youth club near Millwall. We were in kayaks, making our way along a canal and they were fed up with the monotony, dawdling at the back of a field of 200 or so paddlers. We came across a pair of swans with cygnets, taking up about half the width of the canal. The male swan was patrolling the edge of his little family group, gliding back and forth with intent. The lads gingerly made their way past, one at a time, followed by Phil and Ben. Then it was my turn. The voice in my heard wasn't helping,

'Nice one, you've always had a phobia of birds, he'll probably attack you…'

Spot on! The male swan's patience breaks, he's had enough, and comes for me, hissing and snorting, his long neck swollen, wings flapping everywhere, and then I'm in the middle of a mêlée with an angry white beast, ducking and defending myself with my paddle, trying to frantically paddle forward at the same time, the swan landing jabs with his beak and I'm probably screaming, more than once! After a second or two, which feels like a small lifetime, it's all over. He's made his point…

Houseboat man has lost his rag too. He's bellowing at pacer guy in front to

'BE QUIET!'

But pacer guy is carrying on at the same volume,

oblivious, talking his runner through a possible race itinerary for 2023. The South Downs Way 100 is obviously on the cards…

The houseboat man shouts again, this time he's swearing, and for a second or two it runs through my mind that he may have a shotgun. There's a tense hiatus, and then he retreats back into the boat having said his piece.

Shortly after, the first light of Sunday morning is discernible on our port side, and out through the other side of Reading town centre, I dig in with a longer running effort and finally get past the pair, into a clear slot ahead of them. Soon it's light enough for me to experiment with turning the headtorch off.

Someone coming the other way seems to shout 'Hello Gareth!' again. He's gone before I can see who it is. Surely Brian isn't still going on leg four? Could that have been him?

Now when the watch vibrates to tell me another mile is done, amazingly, finally, the number has a lovely nine at the beginning: 90 miles, 91 miles, 91.1, 91.2.

Eventually I'm back at the Tilehurst steps, and then up at the top. Many hours on from our last encounter, I give the 'Welcome to Reading' sign a sarcastic salute, then plod wearily through the housing estate, and head downhill towards the clanging metal gate and the River Thames.

The sun is up. It's a sublime autumnal day, all crystal clear light, sapphire blue sky, the whole valley like a filmset. Across the far side of the river, I kid myself I can make out individual leaves on the low wooded ridge of the Chilterns.

Striding back along the river just after Mapledurham, there's a man coming the other way, clued up, keen to engage, shouting

'YOU'VE GOT SIX MILES TO THE FINISH. JUST

OVER A MILE TO PANGBOURNE.'

It doesn't seem appropriate to blurt out I know this already, I'm fixated with these distances. He means well!

I stride straight past Pangbourne aid station – no need to stop this time - over the bridge, and then dutifully follow the little Thames Path detour round through the churchyard.

Back on the main drag up through Whitchurch-on-Thames, I remember last time I came this way, past midnight in my first 100 mile race, everyone else seemingly asleep. This morning it's flooded with bright redemptive sunlight. An older gentlemen, smartly dressed, is heading home with his Sunday paper.

At the top of the hill, I turn left along a little section of private road through parkland. As I try to march a bit faster, I veer left to pass an elderly looking man with his dog. But he veers over as well, coming towards me, beckoning and eager to chat. Not wanting to be rude I slow down to see what he wants.

'If you're going along the Thames Path, you're about to come across a very steep set of steps…'

Again, it doesn't seem appropriate to let on that I know this already.

'I fought the council to make them safer, told them they were dangerous, that they needed a ramp alongside. I wrote a lot of letters and I won!'

He pauses for dramatic effect…

'I'm Eric Hartley, and they're now known as the Hartley Steps!'

Once I've admired Mr. Hartley's steps (41), and crested the hill on the far side, there's just over three miles to go and it's time to ring Emily to tell her to head to the finish. There's a valedictory feel to the next few miles. I know I'm going to finish between 25 and 26 hours and I can just enjoy the spectacular Sunday morning. All I have to do is put one foot in front of the other.

Down at the bottom of the hill, there's a female competitor moving very slowly indeed. It looks like her pacer is actually her partner and they refuse my offer of help.

Soon I'm making the final left down towards the river - there's just over a mile to go. I stop and take my waterproof off, overheating as the temperature begins to rise. It's almost exactly 12 hours since I put it on, shivering on top of the Ridgeway.

There's the familiar architecture of Brunel's bridge over the Thames, a last brush with the Great Western Main Line. As I get closer to civilisation there are families out for a walk along the riverbank, standard Sunday morning activities.

I've nearly finished, nearly completed the final leg. I'll soon be done tracing out the shape of a 100 mile cross, soon have to step away from this giant adventure playground. This is about the time Emily and I would normally be heading off to church. This has been a kind of church. Just over 25 hours travelling through God's creation on foot, immersed in his landscape and companionship.

Two days out from the race the pain was so strong I'd struggled to walk round the block, and I gave up hope, almost. The Lord answered my request for help: my knee became anaesthetised and held together somehow. I've done my best to honour him in return.

In the week after, when the numbness dissipates, my patella will feel like someone's been bashing it with a hammer, but right now I'm on mile one hundred and there's time to drink in the autumn colours on the slopes opposite, the cloudless sky, the majesty of the gently flowing river alongside. What's that verse again? 'He leads me beside quiet waters.'

Here's the last stretch of towpath into Goring and soon I'm making a right turn and choking back the tears as I wave to Emily, give her a hug and head up to the village hall for the final time.

I stop my personal clock on 25 hours, 11 minutes and 19 seconds. More people than expected have dropped from the race and I end up 105th out of 234 starters...

And I might end it there... if it wasn't for a man called Brian Drought. A gentle and unassuming man who's also something of a colossus. As ever, the Centurion post-race report focuses on the heroics, and frankly incomprehensible athleticism, of those at the front. And in the men's race, Harry Geddes achieves a debut 100 mile win in a stunning time of 14 hours and 52 minutes (42). But towards the back of the field, Brian finishes too. Even though he's done next to no training, even though he only meant to do one leg, even though he's been written off, Brian keeps going, making it to the finish within the cut off time to claim his buckle.

10 CROWHURST

The Autumn 100 is still seven weeks away. Emily and I have come with Neill to Crowhurst Christian Healing Centre (43) for the weekend, and we're sat in the chapel. It's a beautiful late summer evening, just after seven o'clock, Friday 26th August 2022. As ever there's a tangible sense of peace about this place. The doors have been pushed wide open and we can hear birdsong out in the grounds...

It's been a tough week. Andrew, my brother-in-law, a close friend and mentor for over twenty years had been rushed into hospital with breathing difficulties. He's given me a lot of helpful feedback when I've written about running. But the previous weekend he was blue-lighted into hospital, rapidly moved into intensive care and soon he was in an induced coma. Emily and I went up to Barnet to support my sister Heather, who was somehow holding everything together and managing work and the children even though her life had been turned upside down.

When I saw Andrew on the Tuesday afternoon he was unconscious and heavily sedated and breathing through a ventilator. All we could do was play some of his favourite pieces of music on his phone and hope he could hear us.

When we played him 'Jesu's Joy of Man's Desiring', his heart rate, the green line pulsating on the monitor, dropped out of the red for a while, down into the 120s.

As the week progressed it felt like touch and go, that his chances were only 50-50. There was a lot of prayer going on, I was praying, Emily was praying with Heather and Emily's friends were asking for God's help too...

Now we're here at Crowhurst, even though I'm not necessarily one for hearing from God himself, I get a strong sense that he has heard our prayers, everything is in hand and Andrew will pull through.

A blackbird is serenading us from the grounds with a considered and beautiful series of arpeggios. It is sublime. Second by second, I can feel my own pulse rate slowing, a load being lifted from my shoulders.

The three of us had come here for the first time in May, along with a group from the Cornerstone church round the corner from my house in Uckfield. We had found it a refuge, the house and chapel and grounds full of restorative energy. I'd been taken with a particular oak tree, stood tall, at one with its surroundings. And I'd been left with the fleeting idea that my faith could be that grounded and flourishing too.

Here on the Healing Weekend, Steve Gendall the preacher is getting us to find bible verses, then when we're ready, gesturing to each of us in turn, to read our passage out. It's a diverse congregation, and one after another, there are Indian, Afro-Caribbean and English voices to listen to.

"Genesis one, verse thirty-one:
'God saw all that he had made and it was very good'."

"Psalm one hundred and thirty-nine, verse fourteen:
'I praise you because I am fearfully and wonderfully made'"

"Isaiah sixty-four, verse eight:
'We are all the work of your hands'"

"Ephesians two, verse ten:
'For we are God's workmanship created in Christ Jesus.'"

And finally,

"Philippians two, verses twelve and thirteen:
'For it is God who is working in you in order to fulfil his good purpose'"

Steve is teed up. He starts talking in an animated fashion striding back and forth as he speaks.

"You are alive! Isn't that brilliant?

Stop to think about that for a moment. You have five litres of blood continuously pumping around your body - 60,000 miles…"

He pauses and looks over to his wife sat nearby to check he's got the right figure. She nods and he grins and carries on:

"…of capillaries.

How staggering to think your body not only keeps you alive, but helps with your healing. You produce something like 45 billion cells every half an hour and over the next few days many of them will reline your stomach. Without this extraordinary function being repeated, you'd expire! Your body is being renewed all the time."

He's got me thinking about running. These last few months I've had a lot of self-doubt, wondering whether I should even be running at all as a Christian, whether it's actually rather self-centred. The familiar, critical voice in my head has frequently warmed to the task, telling me it's just about making myself look good, a self-interested pursuit of times and medals and 100 mile buckles.

There's a counsellor I respect. After listening to me recounting the hours of effort, the effect on my body of back-to-back long runs, she wonders whether I'm not trying to punish myself somehow, whether there's not a kinder physical activity I can do. I've been wondering if I should pack it all in.

What was it Jesus said?

'I am making everything new.'

Something inside me is triggered and a new insight comes out of the ether. I give myself all the credit for running, for my races and my back to back long runs, but a lot of the time I'm just on autopilot, my mind elsewhere, my legs, my heart and my lungs doing all the heavy lifting for hour after hour. It's beyond comprehension that I've been designed with such care and potential - that doing 100 miles in one go is even possible.

There's another voice in my head. This time it's no longer accusing me. It's full of love.

'This is what I made you to do.'

Since I rediscovered my faith, one of the other parables that's resonated with me the most, is the one about the Talents, the call from Jesus to make the most of the gifts you're given to serve God.

It feels like God is using Steve, and talking directly to me. Running is the gift he's given me. He wants me to glorify him through my running. Actually, it's not selfish at all.

And suddenly, without any warning, I am overcome. God loves me and he loves my running. I hang my head, quietly sobbing, trying not to disturb the others, but brimful of joy.

There's a strong sense of the proximity of the Holy Spirit that's similar to the experience in the Forest with Emily and Neill.

In a one-to-one session with Pippa, an elder from the community - part of the programme the next day - she seems to validate what I felt:

'Maybe you've been looking but not seeing and it's actually quite simple, God wants you to run for him.'

At the end of the weekend Emily goes back to help Heather and I go home and run 21 miles on the Sunday afternoon. When my phone vibrates mid-run with a series of WhatsApp messages I fear the worse, that its bad news about Andrew. But then I feel God gently telling me it's under control. (And sure enough he answers our prayers, Andrew does recover and is able to make it home at the beginning of December.)

Even though my legs feel heavy I'm able to run a gently-paced marathon along the South Downs the day after. I hit a purple patch of running and faith, praying and talking to God as I go, managing 290 miles in the 29 days after the Crowhurst weekend (44).

There will be doubts and tribulations to come of course, not least the troublesome knee injury, which will throw me completely. My faith will flicker on and off as I'm buffeted by daily challenges. And as I start working on my relationship with God longer term, I know full well I'm at the tiny vulnerable seedling rather than mighty oak stage.

However, over the course of the weekend my newly rediscovered belief has been bedded in. And this is reinforced a few weeks later when I have the epiphany moment listening to Amazing Grace on my way to work along London Bridge.

I'm left wanting to put my arms around that lost and restless soul who was searching for so long…

…crossing the narrow rope bridge above the rampaging Braldu River in Pakistan, on his way to K2, playing 'I still haven't found what I'm looking for' volume-up on his Sony Walkman…

…seeking validation through outing after rowing outing at Cambridge, and for a few short months, hitting the heights, the coveted, breathless-38-strokes-per-minute position at the front of the men's first boat for Corpus Christi…

…throwing himself into outdoor pursuits through his twenties and thirties, imagining that climbing E1 or paddling Grade Five, heroically negotiating some multi-pitch mountain route or Alpine river would somehow complete him…

…immersing himself in the pursuit of flow, his poetry, photography, criticised by his Dad for constantly flitting from one thing to another…

…trying to prove something by pushing hard on one fundraising application after another, needing to bring in millions of pounds for London Youth year after year…

…that lost and restless soul, who nearly paid with his life after an error of judgement on the Findhorn, falling off Long Tall Sally, and making a cry for help in the aftermath of Berlin…

…who was actually being looked after all along.

He doesn't need to search any more. He is loved. He is home. Peace has been given unto him.

THANK YOU

I want to acknowledge, and offer a heartfelt thank you to, the following people who helped me during the race, the preparation for the race, at the other times in my life I've described, and in the writing of this book. Especially…

Emily, for loving me, wanting to marry me, supporting me on my journey back to God, understanding my need to run, looking after me on the recce and race weekends, and proof-reading the book.

Ben, for saving my life on the Findhorn.

Matt, for saving my life at Burbage North.

The Centurion staff team and all the volunteers who gave up their time on Saturday 15th and Sunday 16th October 2022 to put on this incredibly well-organised event, not least Stu and Spencer at Goring, Keith at North Stoke, and Jon who gave me my buckle. All of us who took part were looked after wonderfully at the beginning, the end and every aid station in between.

Brian, for always being the living embodiment of the saying 'it's nice to be important, but it's more important to be nice!'

Andrew, for reading and feeding back on a draft of this book.

Louise, for giving me coaching before the race.

Ian, for all his support for my running.

Heather, for being my big sister.

Steve Dewar, for understanding and listening to me, for helping me in the tough times, especially in late 2020, and for encouraging me to write.

Steve Gendall for his inspirational ministry during the Crowhurst weekend.

Michael, for being my running buddy, and German language consultant!

Tony and Pippa, for their support and for encouraging me to write the third book.

Glen for supporting me in the week before the race when all seemed lost because of the knee, for getting into the dot-watching, and for giving me time off at short notice to write the book.

Rosemary, for setting me up with Steve Dewar.

And Zoë, for introducing me to Emily!

REFERENCES

1. *You can find out more here www.morrellroom.org*
2. *This is fairly hard to argue with!*
www.centurionrunning.com/stats
3. *A subject covered in - Gareth Price, 'Duel with the North Downs' (Uckfield: Amazon KDP, 2020)*
4. *www.justgiving.com/fundraising/RunningForOrion. If this page expires, you can also donate via justgiving.com/tommys*
5. *www.centurionrunning.com/news/2022/09/26/tor-des-geants-2022*
6. *www.centurionrunning.com/reports/2015*
7. *Recorded on Strava on 24th and 25th September 2022 www.strava.com/athletes/quietfundraiser*
8. *'Scottish Whitewater. The SCA Guide' (Bangor: Pesda Press, 2001)*
9. *See the excellent descriptions in - Terry Storry, 'British White Water' (London: Constable, 1991)*
10. *Gareth Price, 'One Day by the Thames' (Uckfield: Amazon KDP, 2019)*
11. *www.nationaltrail.co.uk/en_GB/trails/thames-path/25-years/*
12. *Dean Karnazes, 'Ultra Marathon Man: Confessions of an All-Night Runner' (London: Allen & Unwin, 2017)*

13.   *Same as note 10 above*

14.   *Same as note 3 above*

15.   *This one for example*
www.readingmuseum.org.uk/collections/britains-bayeux-tapestry/what-happened-after-hastings

16.   *www.worldhistory.org/article/1318/william-the-conquerors-march-on-london/*

17.   *Many of them are in this definitive guide - Ken Wilson, 'Classic Rock – Great British Rock Climbs' (London: Baton Wicks, 1997)*

18.   *As above – see climb number 36*

19.   *I wrote this from my own memories but it's also covered here www.thebmc.co.uk/a-brief-explanation-of-uk-traditional-climbing-grades*

20.   *Written from my own understanding of the history of the sport rather than any particular book. (Incidentally my Dad said he climbed alongside Joe Brown in the Llanberis Pass in the 1950s)*

21.   *Chris Craggs and Alan James, 'Eastern Grit' (Rockfax, 2006) p211*

22.   *As above p157*

23.   *On here for example*
www.ukclimbing.com/logbook/crags/stanage_plantation-101/namenlos-10163#overview

24.   *Malim, T 2020, 'Grim's Ditch, Wansdyke, and the Ancient Highways of England: Linear Monuments and Political Control', Offa's Dyke Journal, Vol. 2 for 2020, pp. 1-40. (First published in 2007)*

25.   *https://en.wikipedia.org/wiki/Great_Western_Railway*

26.   *Same as note 24 above – page 8 is the relevant part*

27.   *Heavily featured in the photos section on here*
https://www.centurionrunning.com/races/autumn-100-2023

28.   *You can get a flavour here*
www.bbc.co.uk/programmes/p07sxq8c

29.   *Jon blogs under the pseudonym 'Unwilling Veteran' – his 2021 Autumn 100 report is the link below (I found it very useful in the build up to the race) https://unwilling-veteran.sport.blog/2021/10/19/centurion-autumn-100-race-*

report/

30.   Summary here for example
https://en.wikipedia.org/wiki/Robert_Loyd-Lindsay,_1st_Baron_Wantage

31.   See note 4

32.   Dick Francis' racing crime novels were very popular in my house growing up in the 70s and 80s. I remember many of them being set in or around Lambourn and the Berkshire Downs. I found out after the race that Mr. Francis lived in Blewbury a few miles north-east of East Ilsley at the foot of the Downs for many years.

33.   You can relive it here if you would like
https://news.sky.com/story/in-full-boris-johnsons-statement-as-second-lockdown-for-england-announced-12120310

34.   www.soulsurvivor.com

35.   Dane Ortlund, 'Gentle and Lowly. The Heart of Christ for Sinners and Sufferers' (Wheaton, Illinois: Crossway, 2020)

36. For example - Andy Croft and Mike Pilavachi, 'Storylines – Your Map to Understanding the Bible' (Colorado Springs: David C Cook, 2008); Mike Pilavachi and Andy Croft, 'Lifelines – Sound Advice from the Heroes of the Faith' (Colorado Springs: David C Cook, 2008)

37.   Luke 15 verses 11-32

38.   Summary here for example
https://en.wikipedia.org/wiki/Goring_Gap

39.   The story of the Women's race is covered here
https://www.centurionrunning.com/reports/2022/a100-2022-race-report

40.   See note 10

41.   I dare you to google Eric Hartley steps!

42.   Same link at note 39 above

43.   www.crowhursthealing.org.uk/

44.   Recorded on Strava between Sunday 28th August and Sunday 25th September 2022
www.strava.com/athletes/quietfundraiser

ABOUT THE AUTHOR

Gareth Price is a runner and writer currently based in Uckfield in East Sussex. Professionally he fundraises for the charity London Youth as Head of Development.

This is his third book about a 100 mile race. 'One Day by the Thames' and 'Duel with the North Downs' are also available on Amazon in paperback. You can follow him on Strava at www.strava.com/athletes/quietfundraiser

All the author's proceeds from the sale of the book will go to London Youth (registered charity number 303324).

Printed in Great Britain
by Amazon

16813521R00051